# PHAGOPHOBIA: SWALLOW YOUR FEARS

Laugh Your Way to a Healthier
Relationship with Food

Asa Eccleston Kibilski

Copyright © 2024 Asa Eccleston Kibilski

All rights reserved

The characters and events portrayed in this book are fictitious. Any similarity to real persons, living or dead, is coincidental and not intended by the author.

No part of this book may be reproduced, or stored in a retrieval system, or transmitted in any form or by any means, electronic, mechanical, photocopying, recording, or otherwise, without express written permission of the publisher.

# CONTENTS

Title Page
Copyright
Phagophobia: More Than Just a Fear of Swallowing — 1
What's Really Happening: The Science Behind Phagophobia — 3
"It's All in Your Head" … And That's Okay — 6
The Phagophobia Spectrum: From Mild Discomfort to Debilitating Fear — 8
"Just Swallow It!" - Why That Advice Doesn't Help (And What Does) — 11
Laughter as Medicine: The Power of Humor in Healing — 14
The Swallowing Superstars: Your Body's Incredible Teamwork — 17
Mindful Eating: Savoring Each Bite (Without Panicking) — 20
The "Anti-Diet" Diet: Building a Positive Relationship with Food — 22
From Fear to Fun: Rediscovering the Joy of Eating — 25
Food for Thought: Challenging Phagophobia-Related Anxieties — 27
Small Bites, Big Victories: Setting Achievable Goals — 30
The Relaxation Revolution: Stress-Busting Techniques for Phagophobia — 32
The Phagophobe's Toolkit: Essential Coping Strategies — 35

| | |
|---|---|
| Your Support Squad: Building a Phagophobia-Friendly Network | 38 |
| The Professional Touch: When to Seek Help (And What to Expect) | 41 |
| The Phagophobe's Pantry: Building a Fear-Fighting Menu | 44 |
| Mealtime Makeovers: Transforming Fearful Situations into Positive Experiences | 47 |
| Beyond the Plate: Expanding Your World Beyond Phagophobia | 50 |
| Relapse? It Happens: Bouncing Back from Setbacks | 53 |
| Celebrating Success: Recognizing Your Progress (No Matter How Small) | 56 |
| Paying it Forward: Supporting Others on Their Phagophobia Journey | 58 |
| The Future is Bright: Living a Full Life with Phagophobia | 61 |
| FAQ: Your Burning Phagophobia Questions Answered | 64 |
| You've Got This! A Final Pep Talk for Phagophobia Warriors | 67 |

# PHAGOPHOBIA: MORE THAN JUST A FEAR OF SWALLOWING

If you're reading this, chances are you or someone you know has experienced the dreaded sensation of a seemingly harmless bite of food transforming into Mount Everest in your throat. Or perhaps the mere thought of swallowing makes your heart race faster than a contestant on a cooking show facing a surprise elimination. Welcome to the world of phagophobia, the fear of swallowing.

But let's get one thing straight: phagophobia is way more than just a fear of swallowing. It's a complex phobia that can affect every aspect of your life, from your social interactions to your nutritional health. It can make mealtimes a battlefield, family gatherings a source of anxiety, and even the simple act of taking medication a Herculean task.

So, what exactly is phagophobia? It's not just a dislike of certain textures or a picky eating habit. It's an intense, irrational fear triggered by the act of swallowing, often accompanied by physical symptoms like choking sensations, nausea, panic attacks, and even vomiting. It can be triggered by specific foods, liquids, or even pills, and in severe cases, it can lead to avoidance of eating altogether.

Now, before you start Googling "how to survive on an IV drip," let me assure you that there is hope. Phagophobia is not a life sentence. It's a challenge, yes, but it's also an opportunity for growth, resilience, and a renewed appreciation for the simple act of eating.

Think of it like this: your fear of swallowing is like a bully who's been hogging the lunch table for far too long. It's time to stand up to that bully, reclaim your seat, and enjoy your meal in peace.

In this book, we'll dive deep into the world of phagophobia. We'll explore its causes, symptoms, and various treatment options. We'll share tips and tricks for managing your fears, building confidence, and rediscovering the joy of food. We'll even throw in a few laughs along the way, because let's face it, life's too short to be stressed about swallowing.

So, grab a (small, manageable) bite of your favorite snack, get comfy, and let's embark on this journey together. We'll laugh, we'll learn, and we'll conquer phagophobia one swallow at a time.

**Remember:** You are not alone. Thousands of people around the world struggle with phagophobia, and many have successfully overcome it. This book is your guide, your cheerleader, and your culinary companion on the road to recovery.

# WHAT'S REALLY HAPPENING: THE SCIENCE BEHIND PHAGOPHOBIA

Alright, phagophobes, get ready for a crash course in human biology! Don't worry; we'll keep it light, fun, and surprisingly fascinating. After all, understanding the science behind your fear is like shining a flashlight into a dark closet—it might reveal a few dust bunnies, but it also helps you see what's really going on.

Let's start with the star of the show: your throat. This unsung hero of everyday life is a complex system of muscles, nerves, and tissues that work in perfect harmony (most of the time) to ensure that food and liquids make their way safely to your stomach.

**The Swallowing Symphony**

Swallowing is a finely choreographed dance, a four-phase extravaganza involving more than 50 pairs of muscles and nerves. In the first phase, your tongue does a little food-propelling tango, pushing the morsel towards the back of your throat. Then, your soft palate (that fleshy curtain at the back of your mouth) raises like a theater curtain, preventing any unwanted stage diving into your nasal cavity.

Next, the epiglottis (a flap of cartilage that acts like a trapdoor) swings shut over your windpipe, ensuring that your food takes the scenic route to your esophagus (the muscular tube that connects your throat to your stomach) instead of making a surprise detour to your lungs. Finally, your esophagus performs a series of rhythmic contractions, propelling the food downward like a crowd surfer at a rock concert.

**When the Symphony Goes Off-Key**

In people with phagophobia, this finely tuned symphony can hit a few sour notes. The fear response kicks in, triggering a cascade of physiological changes. Your heart rate might quicken, your muscles might tense, and your breathing might become shallow. These changes can make swallowing feel difficult, even impossible, leading to the dreaded choking sensation that is the hallmark of phagophobia.

But here's the thing: it's all in your head. Or rather, it's in your brain. When you experience fear, your amygdala (the brain's alarm system) sends out an SOS signal, triggering the fight-or-flight response. This response is designed to protect you from danger, but in the case of phagophobia, it's like calling the fire department for a burnt piece of toast.

**Your Brain on Phagophobia**

Think of your brain as a computer with a few faulty wires. When you encounter a swallowing trigger (like a certain food texture or the thought of taking a pill), those faulty wires misfire, sending out an inaccurate danger signal. Your brain interprets this signal as a threat, even though there is no real danger, and the fear response kicks in.

But just like you can rewire a computer, you can also rewire your brain. Through therapy, exposure exercises, and relaxation techniques, you can teach your brain to recognize that swallowing is not a threat. You can retrain your fear response, calm your nervous system, and ultimately, regain control over your swallowing.

**The Gut-Brain Connection**

It's not just your brain that plays a role in phagophobia. Your gut, often referred to as your "second brain," also has a say in the matter. Your gut and brain are constantly communicating through a network of nerves, hormones, and neurotransmitters. This gut-brain axis can influence your emotions, your appetite, and even your perception of pain.

In some cases, phagophobia may be linked to gastrointestinal issues like acid reflux or irritable bowel syndrome (IBS). These conditions can cause discomfort or pain during swallowing, which can then trigger or exacerbate the fear response. Treating the underlying gut issue can often help alleviate phagophobia symptoms.

**The Good News**

The science behind phagophobia might seem complex, but it also offers hope. By understanding how your brain and body react to fear, you can develop effective coping mechanisms and treatment strategies. You can rewire your brain, calm your nervous system, and ultimately, conquer your fear of swallowing.

So, the next time you feel that familiar knot of anxiety in your stomach as you raise a fork to your mouth, remember: it's just your brain playing tricks on you. You are in control, and you have the power to retrain your fear response and enjoy food without fear.

# "IT'S ALL IN YOUR HEAD" ... AND THAT'S OKAY

If you've ever been told, "It's all in your head," during a bout of phagophobia, you're likely familiar with the urge to chuck a dinner roll at the offender. But before you start a food fight, let's take a moment to unpack this well-meaning, albeit frustrating, phrase. Because, truth be told, it's not entirely wrong. Phagophobia, like many anxieties and phobias, does originate in your noggin – that wonderful, complex, and sometimes mischievous organ we call the brain.

Now, before you start panicking that you're "crazy" or "making it all up," let's clarify one thing: having a phobia that resides in your head doesn't mean it's any less real or valid. Imagine if you had a broken leg. The pain you feel is very real, even though the source of the problem (your fractured femur) is entirely physical. Phagophobia is similar. The fear, the panic, the physical symptoms —they're all very real, even though the root cause is in your brain's wiring, not a physical obstruction in your throat.

Think of your brain as a high-tech security system, constantly scanning for potential threats and dangers. It's designed to keep you safe, which is generally a good thing. However, sometimes this system gets a little overzealous, mistaking a harmless piece of sushi for a venomous snake poised to strike. This is where phagophobia comes in. Your brain, bless its overly cautious heart, perceives swallowing as a threat, triggering a cascade of fear-based responses that can feel overwhelming.

But here's the good news: just because it's "all in your head" doesn't mean you're powerless to change it. Your brain is incredibly adaptable, capable of learning, unlearning, and relearning. With the right tools and techniques, you can rewire your brain's fear response, calm your nervous system, and ultimately, conquer your phagophobia.

Think of it like this: your brain is like a computer with a software glitch. The glitch (in this case, phagophobia) is causing all sorts of problems, but it's not a permanent hardware issue. With the right software update (therapy, relaxation techniques, etc.), you can fix the glitch and restore your system to its optimal functioning.

In fact, understanding that phagophobia is rooted in your brain can be incredibly empowering. It means you have the ability to take charge of your thoughts, challenge your fears, and rewrite the narrative of your relationship with food. It means you can transform your brain from a fear-mongering bully into a supportive cheerleader, encouraging you to take those brave bites and celebrate every successful swallow.

So, the next time someone tells you, "It's all in your head," smile knowingly and say, "You're absolutely right. And that's why I'm going to conquer it." Because when you embrace the power of your mind, you unlock the potential for incredible healing and transformation. And that, my friend, is not just "all in your head"—it's a reality you can create.

# THE PHAGOPHOBIA SPECTRUM: FROM MILD DISCOMFORT TO DEBILITATING FEAR

If phagophobia were a theme park ride, it wouldn't be a one-size-fits-all experience. It'd be more like a choose-your-own-adventure, with different levels of intensity and a variety of symptoms depending on where you fall on the phagophobia spectrum. Think of it like a spice meter for your fear of swallowing: some folks might experience a mild tingling of anxiety, while others might feel a full-blown five-alarm chili pepper panic attack.

Let's take a tour of the phagophobia spectrum, starting with the milder end.

**Level 1: The Picky Eater's Paradise**

At this level, you might experience a slight hesitation or aversion to certain textures, tastes, or temperatures of food. Maybe you cringe at the sight of chunky peanut butter or gag at the thought of lukewarm soup. You might be a bit of a picky eater, but you're generally able to manage your food preferences without too much distress. Think of it like a gentle breeze on a sunny day – a minor inconvenience, but nothing to write home about.

**Level 2: The Swallowing Skeptic**

As we move up the spectrum, the anxiety intensifies. You might find yourself overthinking every bite, analyzing the texture, temperature, and consistency of your food with the scrutiny of a food critic. You might start to avoid certain foods altogether, opting for safe and familiar options that you know won't trigger your fear. This is like a light drizzle – it dampens your spirits a bit, but you can still function.

## Level 3: The Choking Conundrum

At this level, the fear of choking becomes more prominent. You might experience a tightening sensation in your throat, difficulty swallowing, or even the feeling of food getting stuck. These sensations can be terrifying, leading to panic attacks, avoidance of meals, and significant distress. This is like a steady rain – it's starting to put a damper on your daily life, but you can still find ways to cope.

## Level 4: The Mealtime Meltdown

For those at this level, mealtimes become a major source of anxiety and distress. The fear of swallowing is so intense that it interferes with your ability to eat and enjoy food. You might experience significant weight loss, nutritional deficiencies, and social isolation as you avoid meals and gatherings with friends and family. This is like a thunderstorm – it's disruptive and can cause significant damage, but it will eventually pass.

## Level 5: The Phagophobia Prison

At the extreme end of the spectrum, phagophobia can be completely debilitating. The fear of swallowing is so overwhelming that it consumes your every thought and action. You might become completely reliant on liquid diets, feeding tubes, or even intravenous nutrition. This is like a hurricane – it's devastating and requires immediate intervention.

No matter where you fall on the phagophobia spectrum, it's important to remember that your experience is valid. Your fears are real, and they deserve to be acknowledged and addressed. Don't let anyone minimize your struggles or tell you to "just get over it." There's no shame in seeking help and support.

The good news is that phagophobia is treatable. With the right therapy, support, and coping mechanisms, you can move down the spectrum, reclaim your relationship with food, and rediscover the joy of eating.

So, where do you fit on the phagophobia spectrum? Don't worry if you're not sure. The important thing is to recognize that you're not alone and that there is hope for recovery. This book will equip you with the knowledge, tools, and support you need to navigate your phagophobia journey, no matter where you start.

# "JUST SWALLOW IT!" - WHY THAT ADVICE DOESN'T HELP (AND WHAT DOES)

Ah, the infamous "Just swallow it!" It's the go-to phrase of well-meaning friends, family, and even some healthcare professionals when confronted with someone struggling with phagophobia. It's like telling someone with a broken leg to "just walk it off." While the sentiment might be rooted in good intentions, the delivery is about as helpful as a chocolate teapot in a desert.

Let's dissect why "just swallow it" is not only ineffective but can also be downright harmful for those grappling with phagophobia:

1. It Invalidates the Fear: Telling someone to "just swallow it" dismisses the very real fear and anxiety they are experiencing. It implies that their phobia is a simple matter of willpower, when in reality, it's a complex issue with biological, psychological, and emotional components. It's like telling someone with arachnophobia to "just pick up the spider." It's not that simple, and it's not fair to suggest otherwise.
2. It Increases Pressure: Phagophobia is often accompanied by a heightened sense of self-consciousness and performance anxiety. When someone tells you to "just swallow it," it adds another layer of pressure, making it even harder to perform the already daunting task of swallowing. It's like trying to give a presentation while everyone in the audience is staring at you and whispering, "Don't mess up!" It's a recipe for disaster.
3. It Can Backfire: In some cases, the pressure to "just swallow it" can actually worsen the fear response. Your body might tense up, your heart rate might spike, and

you might start to hyperventilate. Instead of facilitating swallowing, this well-intentioned advice can create a self-fulfilling prophecy of choking and panic. It's like trying to force a square peg into a round hole – it's not going to fit, no matter how hard you push.
4. It Oversimplifies the Issue: Phagophobia is not just a fear of swallowing. It's often intertwined with other anxieties, traumas, or medical conditions. Telling someone to "just swallow it" ignores the complexity of the issue and offers a band-aid solution to a much deeper problem. It's like trying to fix a leaky roof with a roll of duct tape – it might temporarily stop the leak, but it won't address the underlying structural damage.

So, if "just swallow it" isn't the answer, what is? Here are some more helpful and supportive things you can say or do for someone struggling with phagophobia:

- "I understand this is really hard for you." Acknowledging their fear and validating their experience can go a long way in building trust and rapport.
- "It's okay to feel scared." Normalizing their fear can help them feel less alone and ashamed.
- "How can I support you?" Offering practical help, such as researching therapists, accompanying them to appointments, or simply being a listening ear, can make a huge difference.
- "Let's take it one step at a time." Breaking down the process of eating into smaller, more manageable steps can make it feel less overwhelming.
- "You're not alone in this." Reminding them that many people struggle with phagophobia can offer hope and encouragement.

Remember, phagophobia is not a character flaw or a sign of weakness. It's a real and treatable condition. With the right support and guidance, individuals with phagophobia can overcome their fears, reclaim their relationship with food, and enjoy the simple pleasure of eating without anxiety. So, ditch the "just swallow it" advice and offer instead empathy, understanding, and practical support. It's a much tastier recipe for recovery.

# LAUGHTER AS MEDICINE: THE POWER OF HUMOR IN HEALING

Okay, time for a dose of giggles! Grab your funny bone and prepare for a laughter-filled exploration of the healing power of humor, especially when facing the formidable foe of phagophobia.

You might be thinking, "Laughter? Really? How can chuckling at silly jokes possibly help me overcome my fear of swallowing?" But hold onto your hats (and your forks!), because humor is a secret weapon with some surprising superpowers.

**Laughter: The Ultimate Stress Buster**

First and foremost, laughter is a natural stress reliever. When we laugh, our bodies release endorphins – those feel-good chemicals that act as natural painkillers and mood boosters. Endorphins can reduce stress hormones like cortisol, which is often elevated in people with anxiety disorders like phagophobia. Think of laughter as a massage for your mind, relaxing those tense muscles of worry and fear.

Not only does laughter reduce stress in the moment, but it also helps build resilience over time. Studies have shown that people who laugh more often tend to have lower levels of anxiety and depression. Laughter is like a mental shield, helping you bounce back from setbacks and face challenges with a lighter heart.

**Humor: Your Personal Cheerleader**

Humor can also act as a powerful motivator. Think about those hilarious motivational posters with captions like, "When life gives you lemons, make lemonade (and then throw it at someone who deserves it)." They might be cheesy, but they also tap into a universal truth: laughter can give us the courage to face our fears and pursue our goals.

In the context of phagophobia, humor can help you reframe your relationship with food. Instead of viewing mealtimes as a battleground, you can start to see them as opportunities for amusement and enjoyment. Imagine replacing that anxious inner voice with a witty comedian who cracks jokes about your food fears. It might sound silly, but it can actually help to diffuse tension and create a more positive mindset.

**Humor as a Coping Mechanism**

Humor can also be a healthy coping mechanism for dealing with difficult emotions. When we laugh at our problems, we gain a sense of perspective and control. We realize that our fears, while real, don't have to define us or dictate our lives.

Think of it like this: humor is like a pair of comedy glasses that allow you to see your problems through a different lens. Suddenly, that giant, scary sandwich becomes a quirky character in a sitcom, and your fear of swallowing transforms into a running gag. It might not solve the problem entirely, but it can certainly make it feel less overwhelming.

**Laughter as Social Glue**

Laughter is also a social lubricant. Sharing a laugh with others creates a sense of connection and belonging. It can help break down barriers, build trust, and foster a supportive environment.

For people with phagophobia, connecting with others who understand your struggles can be incredibly empowering. Whether it's through online support groups, therapy sessions, or simply sharing a meal with a trusted friend, laughter can create a sense of camaraderie and shared purpose.

**How to Inject Humor into Your Phagophobia Journey**

So, how can you harness the power of humor in your journey to overcome phagophobia? Here are a few tips:

- **Seek out funny content:** Watch a comedy special, read

a humorous book, or listen to a funny podcast. Surrounding yourself with laughter can help lift your mood and reduce anxiety.

- **Find your funny bone:** What makes you laugh? Do you enjoy puns, slapstick comedy, or observational humor? Find the type of humor that resonates with you and incorporate it into your daily life.
- **Share a laugh with others:** Connect with friends, family, or online communities who share your sense of humor. Sharing a laugh with others can amplify the positive effects and create a sense of belonging.
- **Don't take yourself too seriously:** Remember, laughter is about letting go and not taking life too seriously. Allow yourself to be silly, make mistakes, and embrace the absurdity of it all.

While humor is not a cure-all for phagophobia, it can be a powerful tool in your healing journey. So, go ahead and laugh your way to a healthier relationship with food. It's a prescription you won't regret filling.

# THE SWALLOWING SUPERSTARS: YOUR BODY'S INCREDIBLE TEAMWORK

Get ready for a standing ovation, folks, because it's time to shine the spotlight on the unsung heroes of swallowing: your very own body parts! That's right, those seemingly mundane muscles, nerves, and tissues in your mouth, throat, and esophagus deserve a round of applause for their incredible teamwork in the intricate dance of swallowing.

Picture this: a Hollywood blockbuster where a group of misfits with unique talents come together to achieve an extraordinary feat. That's basically what happens every time you swallow, except instead of saving the world from an asteroid, your body parts are ensuring that your delicious slice of pizza reaches its final destination without any unwanted detours.

Let's meet the cast of characters:

- The Tongue: This agile acrobat kicks off the swallowing process by expertly maneuvering the food bolus (fancy term for a lump of chewed food) towards the back of your throat. It's like a skilled juggler, tossing the bolus into the air and catching it with perfect precision.
- The Soft Palate: This flexible curtain rises like a drawbridge, sealing off the nasal cavity and preventing any unwanted food showers in your nose. It's the bouncer of the swallowing world, ensuring that only VIPs (food and drinks) get access to the esophagus.
- The Epiglottis: This flap of cartilage acts as a trusty trapdoor, swinging shut over your windpipe to prevent food from going down the wrong pipe. It's like a vigilant traffic cop, directing traffic and preventing any food-related accidents.

- The Esophagus: This muscular tube is the star of the show, performing a series of rhythmic contractions to propel the food towards your stomach. It's like a conveyor belt at a sushi restaurant, delivering your culinary delights with efficiency and style.

But the swallowing superstars don't work alone. They have a whole team of supporting actors, including your pharynx (throat), larynx (voice box), and various nerves and muscles that coordinate the entire process. It's a symphony of movement, a ballet of biology that happens seamlessly and effortlessly (most of the time).

When Phagophobia Throws a Wrench in the Works

Now, imagine if one of the actors in our blockbuster movie suddenly forgets their lines or trips over a prop. Chaos ensues, right? The same thing can happen with phagophobia. The fear response can disrupt the delicate coordination of your swallowing muscles, leading to a feeling of tightness in your throat, difficulty initiating a swallow, or even the sensation of choking.

It's like a stagehand accidentally tripping over a power cord, causing the lights to flicker and the music to screech to a halt. The actors might stumble, the audience might gasp, and the whole performance might be jeopardized.

But just like a skilled director can salvage a flubbed scene, you can also regain control of your swallowing muscles. Through relaxation techniques, therapy, and gradual exposure exercises, you can retrain your body to perform the swallowing symphony with confidence and ease.

Think of it like physical therapy for your throat. Just as a physical therapist helps you strengthen and coordinate your muscles after an injury, therapy for phagophobia can help you relearn the natural rhythm of swallowing and overcome your fear.

Remember, your body is an incredible machine, capable of

amazing feats. And with the right guidance and support, you can harness that power to conquer phagophobia and reclaim your rightful place at the head of the table. So, let's give a round of applause to the swallowing superstars and cheer them on as they continue their amazing work.

# MINDFUL EATING: SAVORING EACH BITE (WITHOUT PANICKING)

Alright, foodies, it's time to ditch the distractions and embrace the art of mindful eating. Now, before you roll your eyes and think this is just another trendy wellness buzzword, hear me out. Mindful eating isn't about chanting mantras over your muesli or meditating on your mashed potatoes (although, if that's your jam, go for it!). It's simply about paying attention to the present moment, savoring each bite, and tuning into your body's signals of hunger and fullness.

Think of it like this: imagine you're at a concert of your favorite band. You wouldn't spend the entire show scrolling through your phone or chatting with your friend, would you? No, you'd be fully immersed in the music, feeling the vibrations, and singing along at the top of your lungs. Mindful eating is like that, but instead of a concert, it's a culinary symphony, and instead of a band, it's your taste buds rocking out.

So, how can mindful eating help with phagophobia? Well, for starters, it can help you slow down and become more aware of the physical sensations of eating. When you're rushing through a meal, your mind might be racing with anxious thoughts, and your body might tense up in anticipation of the dreaded swallow. But when you slow down and focus on the present moment, you can start to identify those triggers and develop strategies for coping with them.

Mindful eating can also help you tune into your body's hunger and fullness cues. This is crucial for people with phagophobia, who might have developed a distorted relationship with food due to their fear. By paying attention to your body's signals, you can start to re-establish a healthy eating pattern and break free from the cycle of restriction and binging that can often accompany phagophobia.

Now, let's get practical. Here are some tips for practicing mindful eating:

- **Set the scene:** Create a calm and inviting atmosphere for your meal. Dim the lights, put away your phone, and turn off the TV.
- **Engage your senses:** Before you take a bite, pause to appreciate the colors, textures, and aromas of your food. Notice the sounds of your chewing and the way the flavors evolve in your mouth.
- **Savor each bite:** Chew slowly and deliberately, paying attention to the taste and texture of each morsel. Try to identify the different ingredients and appreciate the complexity of flavors.
- **Check in with your body:** As you eat, periodically pause to assess your hunger and fullness levels. Are you still hungry? Are you starting to feel full? Use this information to guide your portion sizes and avoid overeating.

Mindful eating is not about perfection. It's about progress, not perfection. There will be times when your mind wanders, or you find yourself wolfing down your food without thinking. That's okay. Just gently bring your attention back to the present moment and continue savoring your meal.

Think of mindful eating as a muscle that needs to be strengthened. The more you practice, the easier it will become. And the benefits will extend far beyond your plate. You might find yourself feeling calmer, more focused, and more in tune with your body's needs.

So, go ahead and give mindful eating a try. It might just be the secret ingredient you need to transform your relationship with food and conquer your phagophobia.

# THE "ANTI-DIET" DIET: BUILDING A POSITIVE RELATIONSHIP WITH FOOD

Buckle up, buttercup, because we're about to embark on a culinary adventure that will revolutionize your relationship with food. Forget calorie counting, restrictive meal plans, and guilt-inducing cheat days. We're talking about the "anti-diet" diet – a radical approach that prioritizes pleasure, nourishment, and body positivity.

Now, before you start envisioning a diet consisting solely of pizza and ice cream (although, let's be honest, that does sound tempting), let's clarify what we mean by "anti-diet." It's not about indulging in every craving or throwing caution to the wind. It's about rejecting diet culture's harmful messages and embracing a more intuitive and sustainable approach to eating.

Think of it like this: diet culture is like that overbearing relative who constantly criticizes your outfit choices and tells you to "suck it in." The anti-diet is like your cool aunt who encourages you to wear what makes you feel good and dance like nobody's watching.

So, how can embracing an anti-diet mindset help with phagophobia? Well, for starters, it can help you break free from the cycle of fear and restriction that often surrounds food. When you're constantly worried about what you can and can't eat, mealtimes become a source of anxiety rather than enjoyment. But when you give yourself permission to eat intuitively, listening to your body's hunger and fullness cues, you can start to rebuild trust in yourself and your relationship with food.

The anti-diet is also about rejecting the notion that certain foods are "good" or "bad." This is especially important for people with phagophobia, who might have developed a fear of specific textures, tastes, or types of food. When you label foods as "off-limits," you create a sense of deprivation and increase the likelihood of binging or feeling guilty when you do indulge. But when you embrace the idea that all foods can fit into a healthy diet, you can approach mealtimes with a more relaxed and enjoyable attitude.

Here are some key principles of the anti-diet:

- **Honor your hunger:** Eat when you're hungry, stop when you're full. It sounds simple, but it can be revolutionary for people who have been conditioned to ignore their body's signals.
- **Make peace with food:** Give yourself unconditional permission to eat all foods. This doesn't mean eating pizza for every meal, but it does mean letting go of the guilt and shame associated with certain foods.
- **Challenge the food police:** Don't let diet culture dictate what you should or shouldn't eat. Trust your own body and its wisdom.
- **Discover the joy of eating:** Food is meant to be enjoyed, not feared. Experiment with different flavors, textures, and cuisines.
- **Focus on nourishment, not numbers:** Instead of obsessing over calories, macros, or points, focus on choosing foods that make you feel good and provide your body with the nutrients it needs.

Embracing an anti-diet mindset is not an overnight process. It takes time, patience, and a willingness to challenge deeply ingrained beliefs about food and body image. But the rewards are worth it. When you let go of the diet mentality, you free yourself from the shackles of restriction and guilt. You open yourself up to a world of culinary possibilities and rediscover the joy of eating.

So, ditch the diet books, toss out the calorie counter, and embrace the anti-diet revolution. Your taste buds (and your sanity) will

ASAECCLESTON KIBILSKI

thank you.

# FROM FEAR TO FUN: REDISCOVERING THE JOY OF EATING

Alright, phagophobia warriors, it's time to ditch the dread and embrace the deliciousness! If mealtimes have become more of a chore than a pleasure, this chapter is your invitation to rediscover the joy of eating. We're talking about transforming those anxiety-ridden bites into moments of pure culinary bliss.

Now, before you scoff and say, "Joyful eating? With phagophobia? You've got to be kidding!" – hear me out. Yes, I know that food might feel like your enemy right now, but it doesn't have to be that way. Food is meant to be enjoyed, savored, and celebrated. It's a source of nourishment, pleasure, and connection. And even with phagophobia, you can reclaim those positive aspects of food and create a more joyful and fulfilling relationship with it.

Think of it like this: imagine you're on a roller coaster. At first, you might be terrified, clinging to the safety bar for dear life. But as the ride progresses, you start to relax, enjoy the twists and turns, and even let out a few screams of delight. The same can happen with food. It might feel scary at first, but with time and practice, you can learn to embrace the experience and even find joy in it.

Here are some tips for rediscovering the joy of eating with phagophobia:

- **Start small:** Don't try to conquer your biggest food fears right away. Start with small, manageable steps. Maybe it's trying a new food in a tiny portion or experimenting with different textures and flavors. Celebrate each small victory, no matter how insignificant it might seem. Remember, Rome wasn't built in a day, and neither is a healthy relationship

with food.
- **Make it fun:** Eating should be a pleasurable experience, not a punishment. Try incorporating some fun and playfulness into your meals. Use colorful plates and utensils, try new recipes, or have a themed dinner party. Make eating a social activity by sharing a meal with friends or family who support your journey.
- **Focus on the positive:** Instead of dwelling on your fears and anxieties, try to focus on the positive aspects of eating. Notice the flavors, textures, and aromas of your food. Appreciate the nourishment it provides your body and the energy it gives you to pursue your passions.
- **Practice gratitude:** Before each meal, take a moment to express gratitude for the food in front of you. Think about the farmers who grew it, the chefs who prepared it, and the loved ones who might be sharing it with you. Gratitude can shift your mindset from fear to appreciation.
- **Be kind to yourself:** Don't beat yourself up if you have setbacks or bad days. Remember, progress is not linear. There will be ups and downs, but with patience and persistence, you can rediscover the joy of eating.

It might take time and effort, but trust me, it's worth it. When you start to view food as a friend rather than a foe, a whole new world of culinary delights opens up to you. You can explore new flavors, try different cuisines, and share delicious meals with loved ones without fear or anxiety.

So, go ahead and give yourself permission to have fun with food. It's time to ditch the diet mentality, embrace your inner foodie, and savor every bite. After all, life's too short to eat boring food and worry about swallowing.

# FOOD FOR THOUGHT: CHALLENGING PHAGOPHOBIA-RELATED ANXIETIES

Alright, mental gymnasts, it's time to pump up those brain muscles and challenge those pesky phagophobia-related anxieties. We're going to tackle those irrational thoughts head-on and replace them with more positive and empowering beliefs. Think of it like a mental makeover for your food fears.

First, let's identify the culprits: those negative thoughts that pop up like uninvited guests at a dinner party. These thoughts might sound something like:

- "I'm going to choke on this food."
- "Everyone is watching me eat."
- "I'll never be able to eat normally again."
- "This food is going to get stuck in my throat."
- "I'm a freak for having this phobia."

Sound familiar? These thoughts might seem harmless, but they can fuel your anxiety, trigger panic attacks, and make it even harder to overcome your fear of swallowing. It's like having a group of hecklers in your head, constantly booing and jeering at your every attempt to eat.

But here's the thing: these thoughts are not facts. They're just opinions, often based on distorted beliefs and past experiences. It's like a funhouse mirror that distorts your reflection, making you look taller, shorter, wider, or thinner than you actually are.

So, how do we challenge these negative thoughts? It's like playing a game of mental ping-pong. For every negative thought, we serve up a positive, realistic counter-thought. Here are some examples:

- Negative thought: "I'm going to choke on this food." Counter-thought: "I've swallowed food countless times before without choking. My body knows how to do this."
- Negative thought: "Everyone is watching me eat." Counter-thought: "Most people are too busy worrying about their own food to notice mine."
- Negative thought: "I'll never be able to eat normally again." Counter-thought: "Many people have overcome phagophobia and gone on to enjoy food without fear. I can too."
- Negative thought: "This food is going to get stuck in my throat." Counter-thought: "My throat is designed to handle food. Even if it feels uncomfortable, it doesn't mean I'm going to choke."
- Negative thought: "I'm a freak for having this phobia." Counter-thought: "Phagophobia is a common and treatable condition. I'm not alone in this."

Now, challenging negative thoughts is not always easy. It takes practice and perseverance. But the more you do it, the stronger your mental muscles will become. Think of it like training for a marathon. At first, it might feel exhausting and overwhelming, but with consistent effort, you'll build endurance and stamina.

Here are some tips for challenging negative thoughts:

- **Identify your triggers:** What situations or thoughts tend to trigger your anxiety? Once you know your triggers, you can be prepared to counter them with positive thoughts.
- **Keep a thought journal:** Write down your negative thoughts and the counter-thoughts you come up with. This can help you track your progress and identify patterns in your thinking.
- **Practice positive self-talk:** Talk to yourself like you would talk to a friend. Be kind, compassionate, and encouraging.
- **Seek support:** Talk to a therapist or counselor who can help you develop coping skills and challenge negative thoughts.

Remember, your thoughts have power. But you have the power to choose which thoughts you believe. By challenging negative thoughts and replacing them with positive ones, you can rewire your brain, reduce anxiety, and ultimately, conquer your phagophobia.

So, the next time those negative thoughts start creeping in, don't let them take over. Challenge them with the truth, and remind yourself of your strength and resilience. You are capable of overcoming this phobia, one thought at a time.

# SMALL BITES, BIG VICTORIES: SETTING ACHIEVABLE GOALS

Alright, goal-getters, it's time to break down that mountain of fear into manageable molehills! If the thought of conquering phagophobia feels overwhelming, remember this: every journey begins with a single step. Or in this case, a single bite.

Setting achievable goals is like creating a roadmap for your phagophobia recovery. It provides direction, motivation, and a sense of accomplishment as you progress. Think of it like a video game where you level up with each small victory, unlocking new skills and abilities as you go.

But hold your horses, eager beavers! Before you start setting goals like "eat a whole pizza in one sitting" or "swallow a sword" (please don't try that at home), let's talk about what makes a goal achievable.

SMART Goals: Your Phagophobia Power-Ups

The key to setting effective goals is to make them SMART:

- Specific: Don't just say, "I want to get better at swallowing." Get specific. What exactly do you want to achieve? Maybe it's being able to swallow a pill without gagging or enjoying a meal with friends without anxiety.
- Measurable: How will you know when you've reached your goal? Set clear benchmarks for success. For example, "I will be able to swallow a pill with a sip of water three times in a row."
- Achievable: Don't set yourself up for failure by setting unrealistic goals. Start small and gradually increase the difficulty as you gain confidence. It's like starting a workout routine – you wouldn't try to bench press 200 pounds on your first day, right?
- Relevant: Make sure your goals are relevant to your overall

recovery plan. Don't waste time and energy on goals that won't move you closer to overcoming phagophobia.
- Time-bound: Set a deadline for your goals. This will help you stay motivated and track your progress. For example, "I will be able to swallow a pill without gagging by the end of the month."

Example of a SMART Goal:

- Specific: I will be able to eat a bowl of oatmeal without feeling anxious.
- Measurable: I will rate my anxiety level on a scale of 1 to 10 before and after eating the oatmeal.
- Achievable: I will start with a small bowl and gradually increase the portion size over time.
- Relevant: Oatmeal is a soft, easy-to-swallow food that I used to enjoy before my phagophobia developed.
- Time-bound: I will achieve this goal within two weeks.

Breaking Down Your Goals: The Phagophobia Pyramid

Think of your phagophobia recovery as a pyramid. The base of the pyramid is made up of small, manageable goals, like taking a sip of water without gagging or swallowing a bite of mashed potatoes. As you achieve these smaller goals, you build confidence and move up the pyramid to more challenging goals, like eating a sandwich or enjoying a meal in a restaurant.

The key is to take it one step at a time, celebrating each victory along the way. Don't get discouraged if you have setbacks or if progress feels slow. Remember, overcoming phagophobia is a marathon, not a sprint. With patience, persistence, and the right support, you can reach the top of the pyramid and reclaim your life from the fear of swallowing.

So, what are you waiting for? Grab your goal-setting gear and start climbing that pyramid! Remember, small bites lead to big victories.

# THE RELAXATION REVOLUTION: STRESS-BUSTING TECHNIQUES FOR PHAGOPHOBIA

Alright, stressed-out swallowers, it's time to trade in that tension for some tranquility! If your body feels like a tightly wound spring every time you approach a meal, this chapter is your invitation to the relaxation revolution. We're going to explore a variety of stress-busting techniques that can help you calm your nervous system, reduce anxiety, and make mealtimes a more peaceful experience.

Think of your body like a musical instrument. When you're stressed, it's like playing a guitar with rusty strings and out-of-tune pegs. It's hard to make beautiful music when everything is out of whack. But when you relax, it's like tuning those strings and polishing those pegs. Suddenly, your body is ready to create a symphony of calm and tranquility.

So, how do we tune those metaphorical strings and calm that nervous system? Here's a toolkit of relaxation techniques you can try:

1. Deep Breathing: It might sound simple, but taking slow, deep breaths can work wonders for your stress levels. Imagine your breath as a soothing wave, washing away your worries and anxieties. There are many different breathing techniques you can try, like box breathing (in for 4, hold for 4, out for 4, hold for 4) or alternate nostril breathing. Find one that resonates with you and practice it regularly.
2. Progressive Muscle Relaxation: This technique involves tensing and then relaxing different muscle groups in your body. It's like giving your muscles a mini-vacation,

allowing them to release tension and melt into a state of calm. You can find guided progressive muscle relaxation scripts online or create your own routine.
3. Mindfulness Meditation: This practice involves focusing your attention on the present moment without judgment. It's like hitting the pause button on your racing thoughts and tuning into your body's sensations. There are many different types of meditation, so find one that works for you. Even a few minutes of meditation can help you feel more grounded and centered.
4. Guided Imagery: This technique involves visualizing a peaceful scene or scenario. It's like taking a mental vacation to a tropical beach or a serene forest. You can find guided imagery scripts online or create your own. The key is to engage all your senses – imagine the sights, sounds, smells, and feelings of your chosen scene.
5. Yoga and Tai Chi: These gentle exercises combine movement, breathwork, and mindfulness. They can help you improve flexibility, strength, and balance while reducing stress and anxiety. Many yoga and tai chi classes are designed for beginners, so don't be intimidated if you're new to these practices.
6. Humor: We've already talked about the power of laughter in Chapter 6, but it bears repeating. Laughter is a natural stress reliever and mood booster. So, watch a funny movie, read a humorous book, or spend time with people who make you laugh. It's like giving your stress a good tickle – it can't help but loosen its grip.

Remember, relaxation is a skill that takes practice. Don't get discouraged if you don't see immediate results. The key is to find techniques that resonate with you and incorporate them into your daily routine. Over time, you'll notice a shift in your stress levels and a greater sense of calm and well-being.

And who knows, you might even discover that relaxation is

so enjoyable that you start craving it more than your favorite comfort food. Now that's a revolution worth joining!

# THE PHAGOPHOBE'S TOOLKIT: ESSENTIAL COPING STRATEGIES

Alright, intrepid eaters, it's time to gear up with your phagophobia-fighting arsenal! Think of this chapter as your personal toolkit, filled with practical strategies and coping mechanisms to help you navigate the treacherous terrain of mealtimes. We're talking about weapons of mass distraction, anxiety-soothing shields, and confidence-boosting power-ups.

So, put on your metaphorical hard hat, grab your trusty toolbox, and let's get to work building your phagophobia-fighting skills.

Tool #1: The Distraction Dynamo

Sometimes, the best way to conquer a fear is to simply take your mind off of it. That's where distraction comes in. Think of it as your trusty sidekick, ready to swoop in and divert your attention away from those pesky worries and anxieties.

Here are some distraction techniques to try:

- Engage in conversation: Chatting with friends or family during a meal can help you focus on the social aspect of eating rather than the mechanics of swallowing. It's like having a cheering squad at a sporting event, rooting you on with every bite.
pen_spark
- Listen to music or podcasts: Create a playlist of upbeat tunes or listen to an engaging podcast. It's like having your own personal DJ spinning the soundtrack to your culinary adventure.
- Play games or puzzles: Engage your brain in a fun activity like Sudoku, crossword puzzles, or trivia games. It's like giving your mind a mental workout while your body enjoys a delicious meal.

Tool #2: The Relaxation Remedy

As we learned in Chapter 13, relaxation is key to calming your nervous system and reducing anxiety. So, make sure you have a few relaxation techniques in your toolkit that you can pull out whenever you feel your fear starting to rise.

Here are some relaxation remedies to try:
- Deep breathing exercises: Take a few slow, deep breaths, focusing on the rise and fall of your belly. It's like giving your body a mini-massage, soothing away tension and anxiety.
- Progressive muscle relaxation: Tense and relax different muscle groups in your body, starting with your toes and working your way up to your head. It's like giving your body a full-body reset, releasing pent-up stress and promoting relaxation.
- Mindfulness meditation: Focus your attention on the present moment, noticing the sights, sounds, smells, and tastes of your food without judgment. It's like hitting the pause button on your worries and allowing yourself to fully experience the pleasure of eating.

Tool #3: The Confidence Catalyst

Confidence is key to overcoming any fear, including phagophobia. When you believe in yourself and your ability to succeed, you're more likely to take risks, try new things, and overcome challenges.

Here are some confidence-boosting techniques to try:
- Positive affirmations: Repeat positive statements to yourself, like "I am strong," "I am capable," and "I can do this." It's like giving yourself a pep talk, reminding yourself of your inner strength and resilience.
- Visualization: Imagine yourself successfully eating a meal without fear or anxiety. Picture yourself enjoying the flavors, textures, and aromas of your food. It's like creating a mental movie of your success, priming your brain for a positive

outcome.
- Celebrate your victories: No matter how small, acknowledge and celebrate your successes. It's like giving yourself a pat on the back, reinforcing your progress and building momentum for future challenges.

Remember, building your phagophobia-fighting toolkit is an ongoing process. It's like upgrading your smartphone – you'll need to download new apps, update old ones, and experiment with different features to find what works best for you.

So, keep adding to your toolkit, practice your skills regularly, and don't be afraid to experiment with new techniques. With the right tools and the right mindset, you can conquer phagophobia and reclaim the joy of eating.

# YOUR SUPPORT SQUAD: BUILDING A PHAGOPHOBIA-FRIENDLY NETWORK

Alright, social butterflies, it's time to gather your cheerleaders, confidantes, and fellow food adventurers! Overcoming phagophobia is not a solo mission; it's a team effort. Building a strong support network is like having a pit crew for your culinary journey, providing encouragement, guidance, and a helping hand when you need it most.

Think of your support squad as a cast of characters in your personal sitcom. You've got your wise and supportive best friend, your hilarious and encouraging sibling, your knowledgeable and compassionate therapist, and maybe even a quirky online community of fellow phagophobes. Together, they form a dynamic team, ready to tackle any challenge that comes your way.

So, who should be on your support squad? Here are a few key players:

1. Friends and Family: These are your ride-or-dies, the people who know you best and love you unconditionally. They might not always understand your fears, but they're willing to listen, offer a shoulder to cry on, and celebrate your victories with you.
2. Therapist or Counselor: A mental health professional specializing in anxiety disorders can be a valuable asset on your phagophobia journey. They can provide evidence-based therapy, teach you coping skills, and help you challenge negative thought patterns. Think of them as your personal coach, guiding you through the mental and emotional hurdles of recovery.
3. Support Groups: Connecting with others who share your

struggles can be incredibly empowering. Support groups provide a safe space to share your experiences, learn from others, and receive encouragement and validation. It's like joining a club where everyone understands your secret handshake (or in this case, your fear of swallowing).
4. Online Communities: The internet is a treasure trove of information and support for people with phagophobia. There are numerous online forums, social media groups, and blogs where you can connect with others, share tips and advice, and find a sense of community. It's like having a virtual support group that's available 24/7.
5. Dietitian or Nutritionist: If your phagophobia is impacting your nutritional health, a dietitian or nutritionist can help you develop a meal plan that meets your needs and addresses any deficiencies. They can also provide guidance on how to gradually reintroduce feared foods into your diet in a safe and supportive way. Think of them as your culinary consultant, helping you navigate the complex world of food and nutrition.

Building Your Support Squad:

- Reach out to loved ones: Don't be afraid to ask for help. Share your struggles with trusted friends and family members. Let them know how they can best support you on your journey.
- Seek professional help: If your phagophobia is significantly impacting your life, don't hesitate to seek professional help. A therapist can provide you with the tools and strategies you need to overcome your fear.
- Join a support group: Connect with others who understand what you're going through. Support groups can provide a sense of community, encouragement, and validation.
- Explore online resources: There are many online resources available for people with phagophobia. Do some research and find communities, forums, or blogs that resonate with you.
- Consult with a dietitian: If you're struggling with nutritional

issues due to your phagophobia, a dietitian can help you develop a healthy and sustainable eating plan.

Remember, you don't have to go through this alone. Building a strong support network is crucial for your recovery. Surround yourself with people who believe in you, encourage you, and provide the support you need to overcome your fear of swallowing.

Your support squad is like your personal cheering section, rooting for you every step of the way. With their help, you can face your fears, conquer your challenges, and reclaim the joy of eating.

# THE PROFESSIONAL TOUCH: WHEN TO SEEK HELP (AND WHAT TO EXPECT)

Alright, brave souls, it's time to talk about calling in the pros. Now, before you start envisioning a SWAT team bursting through your kitchen door with a plate of mashed potatoes and a therapy dog (although, that would be pretty cool), let's clarify what we mean by "professional help."

We're talking about seeking guidance from trained professionals who specialize in treating anxiety disorders like phagophobia. Think of them as your culinary coaches, personal trainers for your brain, and expert guides on your journey to overcoming your fear of swallowing.

So, when should you consider seeking professional help? Here are a few signs that it might be time to call in the experts:

- Your phagophobia is severely impacting your quality of life: If your fear of swallowing is preventing you from eating a balanced diet, socializing with friends and family, or engaging in activities you enjoy, it's time to seek help. Don't let phagophobia steal your joy and hold you back from living your best life.
- You're experiencing significant distress or anxiety: If the thought of swallowing fills you with overwhelming fear, panic, or dread, it's important to seek professional help. Don't try to white-knuckle it through your anxiety; there are effective treatments available that can help you manage your fears.
- Your self-help efforts aren't working: If you've tried self-help techniques like relaxation exercises, mindfulness, and positive affirmations, but you're not seeing any

improvement, it's time to seek professional guidance. A therapist can provide you with personalized strategies and support to help you overcome your phobia.

- Your phagophobia is affecting your physical health: If your fear of swallowing is causing weight loss, malnutrition, or other health problems, it's crucial to seek medical attention. A doctor can help you rule out any underlying medical conditions and refer you to a specialist if needed.

What to Expect from Professional Help:

Therapy: A therapist specializing in anxiety disorders can help you identify the root causes of your phagophobia, develop coping mechanisms, and challenge negative thought patterns. There are many different types of therapy available, so it's important to find one that resonates with you. Some common approaches include cognitive-behavioral therapy (CBT), exposure therapy, and acceptance and commitment therapy (ACT).

Dietitian or Nutritionist: If your phagophobia is impacting your nutritional health, a dietitian or nutritionist can help you develop a meal plan that meets your needs and addresses any deficiencies. They can also provide guidance on how to gradually reintroduce feared foods into your diet in a safe and supportive way.

Medication: In some cases, medication may be prescribed to help manage anxiety or depression associated with phagophobia. It's important to discuss the risks and benefits of medication with your doctor before starting any treatment.

Support Groups: Joining a support group can provide you with a safe space to share your experiences, connect with others who understand your struggles, and receive encouragement and validation.

Remember, seeking professional help is not a sign of weakness. It's a brave step towards taking control of your health and well-being. Don't let fear or stigma hold you back from getting the support you need.

Think of it like this: if you had a broken arm, you wouldn't hesitate to see a doctor. Phagophobia is no different. It's a treatable condition, and with the right help, you can overcome it and live a full and happy life.

So, if you're ready to take the next step in your phagophobia journey, reach out to a qualified professional. They can help you develop a personalized treatment plan and provide you with the support you need to conquer your fear of swallowing.

# THE PHAGOPHOBE'S PANTRY: BUILDING A FEAR-FIGHTING MENU

Welcome, culinary adventurers, to the phagophobe's pantry! Forget the fear-inducing images of slimy textures and lumpy concoctions. We're about to embark on a gastronomic journey filled with delicious, nutritious, and most importantly, easy-to-swallow foods that will nourish your body and soul.

Think of your pantry as a superhero's hideout, stocked with secret weapons to combat your phagophobia. We're talking about smoothies that swoop in to save the day, soups that soothe your soul, and yogurt parfaits that pack a powerful punch of flavor and nutrition.

But before we start stocking our shelves, let's debunk a few myths about food and phagophobia:

Myth #1: All "Healthy" Foods are Off-Limits

Just because a food is healthy doesn't mean it has to be a choking hazard. There are plenty of nutritious options that are also easy to swallow. Think smooth, creamy textures like avocados, yogurt, and mashed sweet potatoes. These foods are packed with vitamins, minerals, and fiber, making them the perfect fuel for your phagophobia-fighting journey.

Myth #2: You Have to Eat Bland and Boring Food

Phagophobia doesn't have to mean sacrificing flavor. There are countless ways to spice up your meals and make them exciting, even if you're sticking to soft and easy-to-swallow foods. Experiment with different herbs, spices, sauces, and toppings to add a burst of flavor to your plate. Who says mashed potatoes can't be jazzed up with a dollop of pesto or a sprinkle of parmesan cheese?

Myth #3: You Have to Eat Alone

Eating with others can be a powerful antidote to phagophobia. Sharing a meal with loved ones can provide a sense of comfort, support, and normalcy. It can also help you focus on the social aspect of eating rather than the mechanics of swallowing. So, invite your friends and family over for a potluck or join a dining club. Just be sure to choose a restaurant with a menu that caters to your needs.

Now, let's stock that pantry! Here are some phagophobia-friendly food categories to explore:

- Smoothies: These versatile drinks are a great way to pack in nutrients and hydration. Experiment with different fruits, vegetables, yogurt, and protein powder to create your own signature smoothies.
- Soups: Whether it's a creamy tomato soup or a hearty lentil stew, soups are a comforting and nourishing option for people with phagophobia. Just be sure to avoid chunky soups or those with large pieces of meat or vegetables.
- Yogurt Parfaits: These delicious treats are not only easy to swallow but also packed with protein, calcium, and probiotics. Layer yogurt with fruit, granola, and nuts for a satisfying and healthy snack.
- Soft-Cooked Eggs: Scrambled, poached, or soft-boiled eggs are a great source of protein and easy to swallow. Just be sure to cook them to a consistency that you find comfortable.
- Mashed or Pureed Foods: Mashed potatoes, sweet potatoes, avocado, and even fruits like bananas can be easily mashed or pureed for a smooth and satisfying texture.
- Smooth Nut Butters: Peanut butter, almond butter, and cashew butter are a great source of protein and healthy fats. Just be sure to choose smooth varieties and spread them thinly on bread or crackers.

Remember, this is just a starting point. There are countless other phagophobia-friendly foods out there waiting to be discovered. Don't be afraid to experiment and find what works for you. And most importantly, have fun with it! Eating should be a pleasure, not a chore.

So, go forth and conquer your pantry, one delicious bite at a time!

# MEALTIME MAKEOVERS: TRANSFORMING FEARFUL SITUATIONS INTO POSITIVE EXPERIENCES

Alright, culinary warriors, it's time to wave our magic wands (or spatulas) and transform those dreaded mealtimes into delightful experiences! If the mere thought of sitting down to a meal sends shivers down your spine, this chapter is your guide to reclaiming the dinner table and turning it into a haven of relaxation and enjoyment.

Think of mealtimes as a blank canvas. You have the power to paint a picture of joy, connection, and nourishment. But instead of using fear and anxiety as your brushes, we're going to dip into a palette of creativity, mindfulness, and positive energy.

Here are some tips for giving your mealtimes a much-needed makeover:

1. Set the Scene:
- Create a calm and inviting atmosphere: Dim the lights, put on some relaxing music, and light a few candles. Transform your dining area into a sanctuary where you can escape the stresses of the day and focus on the present moment.
- Choose your company wisely: Surround yourself with supportive and understanding people who make you feel comfortable and at ease. Avoid negative energy vampires who might trigger your anxiety. Remember, you're the director of this mealtime movie, so cast the characters who will help you create a positive experience.
- Eliminate distractions: Put away your phone, turn off the TV, and close your laptop. This is your time to disconnect from

the digital world and reconnect with your body and your senses.


2. Focus on the Experience:
- Practice mindful eating: As we discussed in Chapter 8, mindful eating is all about paying attention to the present moment and savoring each bite. Focus on the flavors, textures, and aromas of your food. Notice the way your body feels as you eat.
- Engage your senses: Make mealtime a multi-sensory experience. Use beautiful plates and cutlery, arrange your food artfully, and experiment with different flavors and textures.
- Celebrate the ritual: Transform mealtime into a ritual to be cherished. Light a candle, say a prayer of gratitude, or share a toast with your loved ones.


3. Tackle Triggers Head-On:
- Identify your fear triggers: What aspects of mealtime trigger your anxiety? Is it certain foods, textures, or situations? Once you know your triggers, you can develop strategies for managing them.
- Practice exposure therapy: Gradually expose yourself to your fear triggers in a safe and controlled environment. Start with small, manageable steps and gradually increase the intensity as you gain confidence.
- Use coping mechanisms: Have a few go-to coping mechanisms in your back pocket, like deep breathing exercises, progressive muscle relaxation, or positive affirmations. These tools can help you manage anxiety in the moment and prevent it from escalating.


4. Embrace Imperfection:

- Don't strive for perfection: Mealtimes don't have to be Instagram-worthy to be enjoyable. It's okay if your food doesn't look like a gourmet masterpiece or if you spill a little sauce on your shirt. Remember, the goal is to enjoy the experience, not achieve culinary perfection.
- Forgive yourself for setbacks: If you have a bad day or a meal doesn't go as planned, don't beat yourself up. It's all part of the learning process. Just pick yourself up, dust yourself off, and try again.

Remember, transforming mealtimes from fearful to fun is a journey, not a destination. It takes time, patience, and a willingness to experiment. But with a little creativity and a sprinkle of humor, you can turn those dreaded dinners into delightful experiences that nourish your body and soul.

# BEYOND THE PLATE: EXPANDING YOUR WORLD BEYOND PHAGOPHOBIA

Alright, intrepid explorers, it's time to pack your bags (and maybe a few snacks) and venture beyond the confines of your kitchen! While conquering your fear of swallowing is a major milestone, it's not the end of your journey. Phagophobia might have held you back for a while, but now it's time to spread your wings and explore the world of possibilities that awaits you.

Think of phagophobia as a detour on your life's journey. It might have delayed your arrival at your destination, but it hasn't changed the destination itself. You're still the same adventurous, curious, and passionate person you were before phagophobia entered the picture. It's time to dust off those dreams, rediscover your passions, and create a life that's rich, fulfilling, and fear-free.

Here are some ways to expand your world beyond phagophobia:

1. Embrace New Experiences:
- Travel: Explore new cultures, cuisines, and culinary traditions. Step out of your comfort zone and try new foods that you might have previously avoided. Remember, every bite is an adventure!
- Socialize: Reconnect with friends and family, join a club or group that aligns with your interests, or simply strike up a conversation with a stranger at a coffee shop. Don't let phagophobia isolate you from the people and experiences that bring you joy.
- Pursue Your Passions: What are you passionate about? Do you love art, music, sports, or volunteering? Whatever it is, dive in headfirst and let your passions fuel your journey to recovery. Engaging in activities you love can boost your

confidence, reduce stress, and provide a sense of purpose.
- Learn New Skills: Take a cooking class, learn a new language, or pick up a musical instrument. Learning new skills can challenge your brain, expand your horizons, and give you a sense of accomplishment. Plus, who knows, you might discover a hidden talent you never knew you had!

2. Reclaim Your Confidence:
- Challenge Yourself: Set goals that push you outside of your comfort zone. Whether it's trying a new food, speaking up in a meeting, or taking a dance class, facing your fears head-on can help you build confidence and resilience.
- Celebrate Your Victories: Don't downplay your accomplishments, no matter how small they may seem. Every step forward is a victory worth celebrating. Acknowledge your progress and give yourself credit for the hard work you're doing.
- Practice Self-Care: Take care of your physical and mental health. Exercise regularly, get enough sleep, eat a balanced diet, and engage in activities that bring you joy. When you feel good about yourself, you're more likely to radiate confidence and attract positive experiences.

3. Give Back to the Community:
- Share Your Story: Your journey with phagophobia is unique and valuable. By sharing your story, you can inspire and empower others who are struggling with similar challenges. Consider writing a blog, joining a support group, or speaking at a conference.
- Volunteer Your Time: Helping others can be a powerful way to heal yourself. Find a cause that you're passionate about and volunteer your time and energy. Not only will you be making a difference in the world, but you'll also be gaining a sense of purpose and fulfillment.
- Mentor Others: If you've successfully overcome phagophobia, consider mentoring someone who is just

starting their journey. Your experience and insights can be invaluable to someone who is struggling.

Remember, your life is not defined by your phagophobia. It's a chapter in your story, not the whole book. By expanding your world beyond the plate, you can create a life that's rich, fulfilling, and fear-free. So, go out there and explore! The world is your oyster (or your bowl of ramen, or your plate of tacos – you get the idea).

# RELAPSE? IT HAPPENS: BOUNCING BACK FROM SETBACKS

Alright, resilient readers, it's time for a reality check. Overcoming phagophobia is not always a smooth ride. There will be bumps in the road, detours, and maybe even a few unexpected potholes. In other words, relapses can happen. But before you start panicking and envisioning yourself back at square one, let's reframe this "relapse" as a "setback." It's a temporary detour, not a dead end.

Think of it like this: imagine you're on a road trip to a beautiful destination. You've been cruising along smoothly, enjoying the scenery, when suddenly, you hit a flat tire. It's frustrating, inconvenient, and might even delay your arrival. But it doesn't mean you're never going to reach your destination. You simply change the tire, get back on the road, and continue your journey.

The same goes for phagophobia recovery. A setback doesn't mean you've failed or that all your progress has been erased. It simply means you've hit a bump in the road. But with the right tools and mindset, you can bounce back stronger than ever.

Here's how to handle a phagophobia setback:

1. Acknowledge Your Feelings:

It's normal to feel discouraged, frustrated, or even angry when you experience a setback. Don't try to suppress these emotions. Acknowledge them, allow yourself to feel them, and then let them go. It's like a pressure cooker – if you don't release the steam, it will eventually explode.

2. Analyze the Situation:

Take a step back and analyze what triggered the setback. Was it a particular food, a stressful situation, or a change in routine? Understanding the triggers can help you develop strategies for preventing future setbacks. It's like reviewing game tape after a loss – you identify your weaknesses so you can improve for the next game.

### 3. Practice Self-Compassion:

Don't beat yourself up for having a setback. Remember, everyone makes mistakes. It's part of being human. Be kind to yourself, forgive yourself, and move on. It's like giving yourself a pep talk in the mirror – "You're not perfect, but you're trying your best, and that's what matters."

### 4. Reach Out for Support:

Don't try to go it alone. Talk to a trusted friend, family member, therapist, or support group. They can offer encouragement, perspective, and practical advice. It's like having a pit crew to help you change that flat tire and get back on the road.

### 5. Revisit Your Toolkit:

Remember those coping strategies you learned in Chapter 14? It's time to dust them off and put them to good use. Whether it's deep breathing exercises, mindfulness meditation, or positive affirmations, these tools can help you manage anxiety and regain your confidence.

### 6. Refocus on Your Goals:

Remind yourself of your long-term goals and why you started this journey in the first place. What are you working towards? What do you want to achieve? Refocusing on your goals can help you stay motivated and get back on track.

### 7. Learn from the Experience:

Every setback is a learning opportunity. What can you learn from this experience? What can you do differently next time? Use this setback as a stepping stone to further growth and progress.

Remember, setbacks are not failures. They're simply a part of the journey. By acknowledging your feelings, analyzing the situation, practicing self-compassion, reaching out for support, revisiting your toolkit, refocusing on your goals, and learning from the experience, you can bounce back from setbacks stronger than ever.

So, the next time you hit a bump in the road, don't despair. Take a deep breath, dust yourself off, and keep moving forward. Your destination is still within reach.

# CELEBRATING SUCCESS: RECOGNIZING YOUR PROGRESS (NO MATTER HOW SMALL)

Alright, champions, it's time to break out the confetti and pop the champagne (or sparkling apple cider, if that's more your style)! This chapter is all about celebrating your wins, no matter how small they may seem. Because let's face it, overcoming phagophobia is a big deal, and every step forward deserves a round of applause.

Think of your phagophobia recovery as a marathon, not a sprint. You wouldn't wait until you cross the finish line to celebrate, would you? No, you'd high-five your fellow runners, cheer at the water stations, and maybe even do a little victory dance at each mile marker. The same goes for overcoming your fear of swallowing. Every bite you take without panicking, every meal you enjoy without anxiety, and every food you reintroduce into your diet is a victory worth celebrating.

But here's the thing: we often overlook our small victories, focusing instead on the distance we still have to go. We tell ourselves that our achievements aren't significant enough to warrant a celebration. But that's like saying a single flower isn't beautiful because it's not a whole bouquet. Every petal counts, just like every step forward on your phagophobia journey counts.

So, how do we celebrate our successes? Here are a few ideas:

1. Keep a Victory Journal: Create a journal where you record all your phagophobia wins, big and small. Write down the dates, the foods you conquered, and how you felt. It's like a scrapbook of your journey, documenting your progress and reminding you of how far you've

come.
2. Treat Yourself: Reward yourself for your hard work and dedication. Go for a massage, buy yourself a new book, or indulge in a delicious (and safe!) treat. It's like giving yourself a gold star for a job well done.
3. Share Your Successes: Don't be afraid to share your victories with your support squad. Let them know how proud you are of yourself and how grateful you are for their support. It's like having a cheering section at a sporting event, amplifying your joy and motivation.
4. Practice Gratitude: Take a moment each day to reflect on your progress and express gratitude for your achievements. Gratitude can shift your focus from what you haven't accomplished to what you have, creating a more positive and empowering mindset.
5. Don't Compare Yourself to Others: Everyone's journey with phagophobia is unique. Don't compare your progress to others or feel discouraged if you're not recovering as quickly as someone else. Focus on your own journey and celebrate your own victories, no matter how small they may seem.

Remember, celebrating your successes is not about being vain or self-centered. It's about acknowledging your hard work, reinforcing positive behaviors, and building momentum for continued progress. It's also about giving yourself permission to feel good about yourself and your accomplishments.

So, the next time you take a bite of a food you once feared, or enjoy a meal without anxiety, take a moment to celebrate. Do a little happy dance, give yourself a high-five, or simply say, "I did it!" Because you deserve to be proud of yourself. You're a phagophobia warrior, and you're winning this battle one bite at a time.

# PAYING IT FORWARD: SUPPORTING OTHERS ON THEIR PHAGOPHOBIA JOURNEY

Alright, compassionate comrades, it's time to unleash your inner cheerleader and spread the phagophobia-fighting love! If you've been fortunate enough to make progress on your journey, this chapter is your invitation to pay it forward and support others who are still struggling.

Think of it like this: imagine you're a seasoned hiker who's just conquered a treacherous mountain trail. As you stand at the summit, taking in the breathtaking views, you see a group of novice hikers struggling to make their way up the steep incline. What do you do? Do you ignore them and continue on your merry way? Or do you offer a helping hand, share your knowledge and experience, and maybe even crack a few jokes to lighten the mood?

If you're anything like me, you'd choose the latter. And that's exactly what paying it forward is all about. It's about using your experience, wisdom, and empathy to help others overcome their challenges and achieve their goals.

So, how can you support others on their phagophobia journey? Here are a few ideas:

    1. Share Your Story:

Your story is a powerful tool for inspiration and hope. By sharing your experiences, struggles, and triumphs, you can show others that recovery is possible. You can offer them a roadmap, a glimmer of hope, and a sense of solidarity. Whether it's through a blog post, a social media post, or a conversation with a friend, sharing your story can make a real difference in someone's life.

2. Offer a Listening Ear:

Sometimes, the most powerful thing you can do is simply listen. Let your friend, family member, or fellow phagophobe vent their frustrations, express their fears, and share their triumphs. Be a safe space for them to open up and feel heard. Your empathy and understanding can be a lifeline for someone who feels isolated and alone.

3. Offer Practical Support:

Don't just offer words of encouragement; offer practical support as well. Help your friend research therapists, accompany them to appointments, or simply offer to cook them a meal. Little acts of kindness can go a long way in helping someone feel supported and empowered.

4. Celebrate Their Victories:

Remember how good it felt to celebrate your own successes? Extend that same enthusiasm to others. Celebrate their small victories, no matter how insignificant they might seem. A simple "Congratulations!" or a heartfelt hug can mean the world to someone who is struggling.

5. Educate Others:

Help to raise awareness about phagophobia. Share information on social media, talk to your friends and family about it, or even organize a fundraising event. The more people understand phagophobia, the less stigma and shame there will be surrounding it.

6. Be a Positive Role Model:

Show others that it's possible to live a full and happy life with phagophobia. Don't let your fear define you. Embrace your passions, pursue your dreams, and live life to the fullest. Your example can inspire others to do the same.

Paying it forward is not just about helping others; it's also about helping yourself. When you give back to the community, you reinforce your own recovery and find a deeper sense of purpose and meaning in your life. It's like a boomerang of positivity – the more you give, the more you receive.

So, don't hesitate to pay it forward. Share your story, offer support, celebrate victories, educate others, and be a positive role model. Together, we can create a world where phagophobia is understood, accepted, and ultimately, overcome.

# THE FUTURE IS BRIGHT: LIVING A FULL LIFE WITH PHAGOPHOBIA

Alright, fearless foodies, it's time to look ahead and envision a future filled with delicious possibilities! If you've been living under the dark cloud of phagophobia, this chapter is your ray of sunshine, reminding you that a fulfilling and joyful life is within reach.

Let's be real: phagophobia can feel like a life sentence, a never-ending cycle of fear, anxiety, and restriction. But I'm here to tell you that it doesn't have to be that way. While phagophobia might always be a part of your life, it doesn't have to control your life.

Think of it like this: imagine you have a quirky roommate who always insists on wearing mismatched socks and singing off-key show tunes in the shower. At first, it might be annoying, even frustrating. But over time, you learn to accept their quirks, laugh at their antics, and even find a strange fondness for their off-key singing. Phagophobia can be like that quirky roommate. It might always be there, lurking in the background, but it doesn't have to ruin your life.

Here's how to create a bright future with phagophobia:

1. Redefine Your Relationship with Food:
- Focus on nourishment: Shift your focus from fear to nourishment. See food as fuel for your body, a source of energy that allows you to pursue your passions and live your best life.
- Embrace pleasure: Don't be afraid to enjoy food! Savor the flavors, textures, and aromas. Let yourself indulge in your favorite treats (in moderation, of course).
- Practice gratitude: Be thankful for the abundance of food available to you. Remember, not everyone has the privilege of

choosing what they eat.

2. Set New Goals:

- Don't let phagophobia hold you back: Phagophobia might have put some of your dreams on hold, but it's not too late to pursue them. Set new goals that excite and challenge you. Whether it's traveling to a new country, starting a new hobby, or simply trying a new recipe, don't let fear dictate your life.
- Break down your goals into smaller steps: Rome wasn't built in a day, and neither is a life free from the constraints of phagophobia. Break down your goals into manageable steps and celebrate each milestone along the way.
- Don't be afraid to ask for help: If you're struggling to set or achieve goals, don't hesitate to seek help from a therapist, coach, or mentor. They can provide guidance, support, and accountability.

3. Build a Supportive Community:

- Surround yourself with positive people: Choose to spend time with people who uplift and encourage you. Avoid those who trigger your anxiety or make you feel ashamed of your struggles.
- Connect with other phagophobes: Joining a support group or online community can be a lifeline for people with phagophobia. It's a place where you can share your experiences, learn from others, and receive encouragement and validation.
- Be an advocate for yourself: Don't be afraid to speak up about your needs and advocate for yourself. If a restaurant doesn't have any phagophobia-friendly options on the menu, ask if they can make a modification. If a friend or family member makes a insensitive comment about your eating habits, gently educate them about phagophobia.

Remember, your future is not determined by your past. You have the power to create a life that is full of joy, purpose, and delicious food! Embrace your quirks, celebrate your victories, and never give up on your dreams.

And who knows, maybe one day you'll be sharing a plate of sushi with your phagophobia, laughing about the old times when it used to control your life. Now that's a future worth fighting for!

# FAQ: YOUR BURNING PHAGOPHOBIA QUESTIONS ANSWERED

Alright, curious minds, it's time for a Q&A session! In this chapter, we're going to tackle some of the most frequently asked questions about phagophobia. We'll delve into the nitty-gritty details, debunk myths, and offer some practical advice to help you navigate the often confusing world of this phobia. So, grab your magnifying glass and let's get to the bottom of these burning questions:

Q1: Is Phagophobia a Real Thing?

Absolutely! Phagophobia is a recognized anxiety disorder characterized by an intense fear of swallowing or eating. It's not just a matter of being a "picky eater" or having a sensitive gag reflex. It's a real condition that can significantly impact a person's quality of life.

Q2: What Causes Phagophobia?

There's no single cause of phagophobia. It can be triggered by a variety of factors, including:

- A traumatic experience: A past choking incident, a negative experience with food poisoning, or even witnessing someone else choke can trigger phagophobia.
- Underlying anxiety or panic disorder: People with anxiety or panic disorder may be more prone to developing phagophobia.
- Genetics: Some research suggests that phagophobia may have a genetic component.
- Learned behavior: Children who grow up in households where food is a source of stress or anxiety may be more likely

to develop phagophobia.

Q3: What Are the Symptoms of Phagophobia?

Phagophobia symptoms can vary from person to person, but some common ones include:

- Intense fear or anxiety when swallowing or eating
- Choking sensation or feeling of food getting stuck in the throat
- Nausea, vomiting, or gagging
- Avoidance of certain foods or textures
- Panic attacks
- Weight loss or malnutrition

Q4: Is Phagophobia Treatable?

Yes! Phagophobia is a treatable condition. With the right therapy, support, and coping mechanisms, most people with phagophobia can significantly reduce their fear and anxiety and improve their quality of life.

Q5: What Are the Treatment Options for Phagophobia?

There are a variety of effective treatment options available for phagophobia, including:

- Cognitive-behavioral therapy (CBT): This type of therapy helps you identify and challenge negative thought patterns that contribute to your fear of swallowing.
- Exposure therapy: This involves gradually exposing yourself to your fear triggers in a safe and controlled environment.
- Relaxation techniques: Deep breathing exercises, progressive muscle relaxation, and mindfulness meditation can help reduce anxiety and improve your ability to swallow.
- Medication: In some cases, medication may be prescribed to help manage anxiety or depression associated with phagophobia.

Q6: Can I Overcome Phagophobia on My Own?

While some people are able to manage their phagophobia with self-help techniques, most people benefit from professional guidance and support. A therapist can help you develop personalized coping strategies and provide a safe space to explore your fears and anxieties.

Q7: What Can I Do to Support a Loved One with Phagophobia?

If someone you love has phagophobia, the most important thing you can do is offer them your support and understanding. Avoid criticizing their eating habits or pressuring them to eat foods that trigger their anxiety. Instead, offer encouragement, listen to their concerns, and help them find resources and support.

Remember, phagophobia is a real and treatable condition. If you're struggling with this phobia, don't be afraid to seek help. With the right support, you can overcome your fear of swallowing and enjoy food again.

# YOU'VE GOT THIS! A FINAL PEP TALK FOR PHAGOPHOBIA WARRIORS

Alright, fearless foodies, we've reached the final chapter of our culinary adventure. You've learned about the science behind phagophobia, explored various coping mechanisms, and discovered the power of a positive relationship with food. Now, it's time for one last pep talk before you continue on your journey to conquering this fear.

First and foremost, I want you to know that you are not alone. Thousands of people around the world struggle with phagophobia, and many have successfully overcome it. You are strong, capable, and resilient. You have the power to overcome this challenge and reclaim your life.

Remember, phagophobia is not a character flaw or a sign of weakness. It's a real and treatable condition. Don't let anyone tell you otherwise. Don't let shame or stigma hold you back from seeking help and support. You deserve to live a life free from fear and anxiety.

As you continue on your journey, remember these key takeaways:

- Phagophobia is a journey, not a destination: Recovery takes time, patience, and perseverance. There will be ups and downs, but don't give up. Celebrate your victories, learn from your setbacks, and keep moving forward.
- You are not defined by your phobia: Phagophobia is just one aspect of your life. It doesn't define who you are or what you're capable of. Don't let it limit your dreams or hold you back from living your best life.
- You have the power to change your brain: Your brain

is incredibly adaptable. With the right tools and techniques, you can rewire your fear response, calm your nervous system, and create new, positive associations with food.
- There is no shame in seeking help: If you're struggling, don't hesitate to reach out to a therapist, support group, or loved one. There's no shame in asking for help. In fact, it's a sign of strength and courage.
- You are not alone: Thousands of people are rooting for you. You have a whole community of fellow phagophobes who understand your struggles and want to see you succeed.

So, what are you waiting for? It's time to take everything you've learned in this book and put it into practice. It's time to face your fears, challenge your negative thoughts, and rediscover the joy of eating.

Remember, you are not just a phagophobe. You are a warrior, a survivor, a champion. You have the strength, courage, and resilience to overcome this challenge and create a life that is full of joy, purpose, and delicious food.

So, go forth and conquer! Take that first bite, try that new recipe, and share a meal with loved ones. Don't let fear hold you back any longer. The world is your oyster (or your bowl of ramen, or your plate of tacos – you get the idea).

And remember, I'm always here cheering you on, every step of the way. You've got this!

Printed in Great Britain
by Amazon